MAKE MONEY FROM PROPERTY

BRISTOL FASHION

DEL BROWN

First published 2012 by Tangent Books
Unit 5.16 Paintworks
Arnos Vale
Bristol
BS4 3EH

0117 972 0645

www.tangentbooks.co.uk

Publisher: Richard Jones
Richard@tangentbooks.co.uk

ISBN 9781906477660

Copyright: Del Brown

Editor: Marc Leverton (marcleverton@yahoo.co.uk)

Design: Joe Burt (joe@wildsparkdesign.com)

Print management: Jonathan Lewis (essentialprintmanagement@gmail.com)

A CIP record for this book is available from the British Library

Printed in the UK using paper from a sustainable source.

THANK YOUS!

To my Mum and Dad, Mae & Lesley Brown for all the hard work of bringing us up and always being there for us - even now, as my inspiration and good values would not be there without you.

Thank you to my brothers and sister, Dave, Steve and Sonia for keeping a tight family unit as this has been essential for me in having good stability in building my life. It's always good to be able to rely on my family for any constructive criticism.

Thank you to Nicola my partner for being there and putting up with my constant business talk. Through all the ups and downs, bad times and good you have encouraged and backed me all the way.

Big thanks to my two daughters, Tiana and Chanel for bringing me back down to reality, bearing with me and understanding when I cannot spend enough time with them due to all the business commitments. Without you both the extra inspiration would not have been there to work hard for you.

Thanks to Marc Leverton for helping me put this first book together, I was so pleased to find you and hopefully this will be the start of many more books.

CONTENTS

STARTING OUT IN THE PROPERTY BUSINESS

INTRODUCTION

Thank you for buying this book. I am Del Brown. I am not famous, but I am fairly well known for creating various successful property businesses in my home town of Bristol.

I had a very humble beginning in life. My family came to the UK from Jamaica in search of a better life in the 1960s. They worked hard and we had a small house in a working class area of Bristol, Bedminster. We had to work hard to make ends meet; I am sure that will be a similar kind of background to many of you reading this book.

My aim is to tell you of my own journey, warts and all, the successes and the mistakes. And trust me – there are plenty of those!

WHAT IS BRISTOL FASHION?

Back in the day, 'Bristol fashion' meant having your vessel 'ship-shape'. Although I like things to be ship-shape, what I am really stressing is the need to take a positive kind of approach.

Nowadays I come across lots of entrepreneurial types trying to get ahead, whether through buy-to-let, getting their kids on the property ladder or creating property portfolios using lease options.

So now I take 'Bristol fashion' to mean *hustling* for business, doing deals, trying to create more income for yourself now and for the future. Of course, this happens everywhere, but I am from here and know the Bristol market. I hope you can take the lessons I have learned here and apply them elsewhere.

ABOUT THIS BOOK

People always ask me for the secret to my business success. The truth is, there are no secrets. There is nothing 'secret' that someone else could not find out about or pick up.

I have made a lot of money from the property business, that much is true. The 'secrets' are basically hard work, building up your *own* business rather than someone else's, and not being afraid to make mistakes. Plus, I have educated myself along the way: self-education is very important.

This book will show you how to get into property; there are many routes, not just the well known ones such as buy-to-let. I will also share my experiences of property management, plus some thoughts on general business management.

This book isn't an autobiography, although I am happy and proud to share with you some of my early experiences and thoughts. I have done this because I know people like to know who they are dealing with, and I also think real-life examples are more useful than theoretical principles.

I mentioned my humble family background. As well as this, I left school with only five CSEs, and started working on building sites in the 1980s after completing a Carpentry Apprenticeship at Brunel Technical College.

I have achieved more than I ever dreamt possible – and I genuinely believe anyone can do what I have done, or at least part of it. I know it is a bit of a cliché to say 'If I can do it, you can too'. So let's just say I would like to see more people take control of their financial futures, and this book is written to help you achieve that.

I have broken it into sections. The first part is about my own journey, my 'rags-to-riches' tale, if you like. I then go on to discuss inspiration, and in Part Three we get on to the nitty gritty, focusing on my business of property and telling you how *you* can make money from it, too. There are lots of practical bits of advice in here, lots of tricks of the trade – all valuable information that has taken me years to accumulate.

I believe it takes great teams to achieve big things; even the very best individuals need great people around them. So in Part Four I share the inspirational coaching messages that have helped me make the transition from builder to businessman.

Finally, Part Five is more on the day-to-day property business methods which I think are important. I hope lots of property people read the book, but I also hope I have advice to give which will reach out into the wider business community.

So far I have told you *what* you will find in this book, but I haven't explained *why* I am writing it. I have reached the luxurious position in which if I wanted to, I could stop working. I have enough money. But I *do* keep working, because I love to work and I love the world of business.

Right now, in 2012, the world is going through so many changes, and people are living in fear of their jobs. Life has become a lot more unpredictable. I want to show people how to make their futures more secure. I want to show them that going to work doesn't need to be a chore. Mostly, I want to help you get more control over your lives, and ultimately enjoy life more. We are only on this planet for a short time; let's make the most of it!

Del Brown, Bristol, 2012

MY STORY

My parents came to the UK from Jamaica in the early 1960s, part of that first wave of immigrants who thought they were coming to the land of plenty. They were in for a bit of a shock. They moved to Bristol as my dad had a brother here, and we all lived together. I was born in 1963, one of four kids.

My parents had to work two jobs, day and night, to make ends meet. Our first place was in Mendip Road, with the whole family in just one room! My mum had various jobs as an auxiliary nurse at local hospitals, and dad did everything from cleaning to engineering work.

Between them, my parents and my uncle managed to save enough money to buy a small house in Mendip Road, Bedminster, a working-class area with traditional two- and three-bedroom terrace houses south of the river Avon.

It is interesting looking back at this, now, because times were tough and we had to work hard to get ahead. But times are also tough right now, and one of the trends I am seeing in the property market today is people looking for more family help. What was true then is true now. You can still get on, but it requires either a bit of creative thinking, some help from family and friends – plus, of course, some old-fashioned graft!

I think the struggle my parents had has given me my entrepreneurial side. They were never frightened of hard work and tried to get on where they could, and this is exactly what I have done in my career.

Another aspect of my home life which shaped who I am today is that from about 14 years old I started wanting my own money. Knowing my parents were working several jobs, I did not want to ask them for money. Instead, I started finding working part-time, everything from a mechanic's mate to a butcher's boy.

School

I didn't enjoy school that much at first. I was quite shy and found it hard to make friends. Thankfully, it was through sport that I found a way to express myself, and I discovered I had a real talent for it, too. I liked all sports, but especially football and athletics.

Getting into sport made me more popular with the other kids, and that helped me keep the bullies away. I got so fast that I was picked to run for Bristol. I had my own trainer, won some trophies and was even featured in the local newspaper for winning competitions. I loved it so much, and it was through sport that I started to develop my competitive side. Football in particular taught me about teamwork, and you will see later that I am still very much a team player.

In my teens I also got into boxing, I was one of those millions of young kids who was inspired by Muhammad Ali. I got quite good at it, but my heart wasn't really in it.

I think sport encapsulates so much that also applies to business. Think about how competition, teamwork, strategy, inspiration, creativity and management all have a role in both worlds; I'll expand on this later in the book.

Early days of work

I left school with only five CSEs and no direction, and with some shoving from my dad I eventually drifted into carpentry and found work on building sites. It was very repetitious and boring. I'd have to hang hundreds of doors or lay hundreds of feet of timber noggins. Not only was it hard, it was also piece work, which meant I would get paid by the metre – but although I didn't appreciate it at the time, I was building some knowledge that would prove to be very handy later on.

My first business, SOS building services
From casual work on building sites I built up my own building business over the next 10 years. I was supplying construction services to organisations such as housing associations, the council and some private developers, and eventually I got to the stage where I was employing 18 people and we were working on lots of properties. The downside was that I was working really long hours. I wasn't happy, and it was so stressful that I got to a point where my hair started falling out!

I was chasing payments all the time, constantly worrying about the work other people were doing, feeling over-reliant on them, so never in control of what was happening. On top of all that, the business was just not making money – so one day, I just decided to quit it all.

My second business, DB Properties
Although you could argue that my first venture was a property business, I never considered myself to be working in that world until I made a conscious decision to do so and set up DB Properties.

I had bought and sold my first house in 1992 and had made a good profit, too, of nearly 25 per cent. This was with very little experience in raising credit, and without a clear strategy.

It was in 1997 that I decided to try going into property with the intention of making my living from it. I had no idea how far it would go, but I realised pretty quickly that buying and selling properties ('flipping') was a much less stressful way to make a living than what I had been doing. I was helped along the way by the strength of the market, which was on the up, and by the fact that I had many necessary contacts from my previous building company.

From 1998 to 2002 I invested in a wide range of properties, and while I sold many of them on for a profit, I also kept quite a few to rent to tenants. It was this that gave me my next idea.

My third business, property agency Liv'N'Let

By 2002 I had a group of properties that I was letting out. Things were going quite well, but I was still working very hard and spending a lot of time running around town trying to keep on top of things.

I couldn't help but feel the business could be better. A new problem starting to emerge that the letting agencies weren't promoting my properties very well. This was incredibly frustrating: they weren't really doing their job, but you can't get too shirty with them as you need to keep them onside.

I hit upon the idea of starting my own letting agency, so that I could promote my properties in the way I thought best. I clearly remember thinking: *'How hard can it be?'*

Truth be told, it wasn't and still isn't that difficult. The key component I needed, which I found quite quickly, was a database. There are databases tailor-made to letting agencies, and these take a lot of the stress and hard work out property letting. Most importantly, the database povided all the structure I needed to stop worrying, giving me the mental space to start thinking of things other than the day-to-day running of my let properties.

Up to this point I was always trying to juggle 10 things in my head at once. I had notebooks with lists of things to keep on top of – which property needed which bit of work, who owed me rent, who I needed to get a reference for – all those little bits and pieces which build up into a mountain of administration very quickly. By setting up the property letting business and taking on extra responsibility, I had actually managed to make my life easier; life was looking up again.

Now, 10 years later, my lettings agency employs five people. I have over a hundred units (flats and houses) being let out through Liv'N'Let, plus I am letting out other landlords' properties, too.

Well, that's enough about Del Brown. This isn't about me bragging about what I have achieved – but I *do* want you to know that you are reading a book by someone who has been there and done that.

The key ingredients to my success (and yours)

- Vision
- Determination
- Be willing to do whatever it takes
- Don't worry about making mistakes
- People Skills
- Know your market

One of the reasons I like working in this sector is that property has no face. It doesn't matter whether you are short, tall, female, male, black or white. As long as you can show the money, you can have any property you want.

WHY GO INTO BUSINESS?

Business is at the heart of everything, and making a deal is at the heart of business. Every time we go out to eat, turn the television on, meet friends for a coffee or buy our houses, we are helping the wheels of business to turn.

I started out with nothing, and part of the attraction has been building up something out of nothing. I had no access to credit or money and had to beg and borrow to manage my first detail.

There is a famous book written by Robert Kiyosaki called *Rich Dad, Poor Dad.* In it, he says that if you want to free yourself from the nine-to-five rat race, you need to go into business. Otherwise you will always be a wage slave.

I want the freedom to be doing things because I *want* to, rather then *need* to. It may seem like a dream, but it isn't as hard as you might think. I don't have any educational qualifications beyond five CSEs and I don't have any formal business training. I know it is a cliché but honestly, if I can do it, anyone can.

It may seem from a distance that setting up a business is hard work and there are lots of risks involved. But a bit of risk can really focus the mind, and it also gets you out of bed in the morning. I know that if something goes wrong, it is down to me. I also know that if something goes well, that is also down to me.

I see people look at me sometimes and I can almost read their minds. They are saying 'I wish I could do that, but I can't', and then they carry on with the day-to-day drudgery of going to work in a job they hate. Trust me, it is harder to do that than it is to get up in the morning and get on with something you are really passionate about.

WHAT IS PROPERTY INVESTMENT?

The underlying factor to successful property investment is making a profit. At the time of writing in 2012, the market is still holding up; although it isn't as buoyant as it has been in the past, the value of property is still good.

Essentially, if you can buy a property and sell it at a profit, you are in business. If you can buy a property and rent it out making a profit, you are in business.

It is still possible to find what is termed a *below market value* property. People may want to sell a house at BMV for the following reasons:

- The current owners have got into financial difficulty, and it is better for them to sell quickly and take some of their equity rather than lose it to the bank.
- The house has been repossessed already, and the new owner wants a quick sale.
- The house has been inherited, and the new owner wants a quick sale.

As all the world's markets face tough times, the nature of investment is changing to reflect this. People are investing together to reduce the risks, so now we are starting to see property clubs forming. One of the great things with groups of people working together is that it *lowers the entry level* for people wanting to invest.

Despite the recession, or perhaps because of it, property is still a good long-term investment. There remains a shortage of property in the UK, and this keeps prices good. Obviously, they have come down from a peak in 2007, and the market might have slowed, but there is still enough going on for people to get involved.

THE BRISTOL MARKET

In the first months of 2012 the Bristol property market was still very strong. We are lucky that in the city we are beating the national trend of cooling prices, which have seen valuations drop as much as 20 per cent in some places.

The drop in Bristol since the peak of 2007 is possibly around 2 per cent overall, but some hotspots remain and there is still a profit to be made by homeowners and developers alike.

During the recession of the early 1990s Bristol again got away relatively unscathed, and there are several good reasons for this. The jobs market here is consistently steady, with a mixture of industries. And importantly for readers of this book Bristol has a very *strong rental market,* which I'll come back to. The infrastructure of the city is good, we are close to the M4 and M5 and have two major stations with good rail links to London and the rest of the country.

With prices in Bristol strong, the challenge for many first-time buyers is getting a foothold on the ladder, and this book will examine various techniques for doing this.

The national average house price in 2012 is £233,252. In Bristol it is £207,669 – but these figures don't tell the whole story. What we have here is a market place akin to London in that there are vast differences in prices, depending upon location.

Largely speaking, the property market increases in value from east to west, so prices are lower in such areas as Easton, St George and Whitehall. Then, across the M32, heading west into the more fashionable areas of St Werburghs and Montpelier, the prices start rising a bit before, continuing further west, we hit the peaks of

Cotham, Redland, Clifton and Westbury. Besides that east to west trend, parts of south Bristol also boomed in the early 90's, creating new hotspots such as Southville.

The strong rental market in Bristol is largely fuelled by the two universities, strong graduate employment opportunities for young professionals and international industries such as Aerospace and Rolls Royce which bring skilled workers to the city. All these factors keep the rental market ticking over.

The future looks good, too, with major projects continuing to be announced: investment in hospitals, schools, a new enterprise zone, a new science park and the like. In essence, Bristol has continued to hold up despite the global recession which has seriously knocked the wind out of many places. If you are reading this outside Bristol, I recommend that you research your own market thoroughly, look at the history of prices and analyse the market place.

If you are in Bristol, know that you are lucky to be living in the ideal place to make an investment in the property market, whether you are thinking of buy-to-let or planning something more ambitious.

PART

2

HOW TO BUILD PROPERTY PROFITS FROM SCRATCH

This is the part of the book where I want to give you some of the nitty gritty details that will help you either acquire your first property or help you build a property-based business.

I will show you:
- Where property profits come from
- How to manage private rentals
- Different types of investment
- How to raise finance
- How to find a property
- How to sell a property

I aim to show that everyone can understand how this whole process works. I don't want anyone to feel that the property business isn't something they can work in.

When you meet some sharp person in a suit and they tell you they work in property, they could be talking about being anything from a labourer to an investor. By the end of this section you will know what is what in property, and I hope will be able to make some decisions about the right way forward for you.

When thinking about making an investment we need to weigh up our personal factors against what the market is offering. These factors influence what our strategy will be and help us develop the niche that works for us.

I have been working in property for nearly 25 years and have personal experience of all of the areas below. Over the next few pages I shall introduce you to the most common areas people choose to specialise in, and I hope this will enable you to make an informed decision on which option best suits you.

WHERE DO PROPERTY PROFITS COME FROM?

FLIPPING PROPERTIES

Flipping is buying and re-selling a property, preferably quickly. This is the classic Sarah Beeney *Property Ladder* stuff on Channel 4, and was how I did my first few deals.

Take my first deal (in 1992):

£13,000 cost of property
£3,000 spent on renovations
£21,000 selling price
£5,000 profit

And a recent example in today's prices:

£145,000 cost of property
£25,000 spent on renovations
£210, 000 selling price
£40,000 profit

The first example is an illustration from 'the good old days' when property flipping was easy and the profits were almost guaranteed. There are still places in the country where you can flip – yes, even now, in the middle of a recession, and here are my *top tips for finding a property ideal for flipping*:

- You need to do your research, and find the *right property* in the *right place*. Remember that old mantra: 'location, location, location'.
- Is the market still strong in your area? An interesting aspect of the recession is that it is hitting harder in different areas. Keep your eyes peeled on how long properties are taking to sell.
- You really need to know your area. Check out the schools – are they attracting young families into the area?
- Are there any proposed developments which are going to change

the market?
* What kind of properties are popular with your target market?
* Is the property for shared occupancy or for families?
* Is a garden important? Does it need tidying up?
* Are there local universities nearby? A large local employer?
* Do these factors influence who your target tenant will be?
* In your search for a property to flip you need to trawl through lots of property websites. www.rightmove.co.uk, www.findaproperty.com and www.zoopla.co.uk are among the more obvious ones, and then, of course, there are all your local estate agents' sites.

But don't rely just on the internet, Speak to estate agents, because if you can find one who is willing to share some local knowledge, it could save you a lot of leg work.

By the time a property is on the estate agents' websites and in their windows it is on the open market, there for all to see. But there is another market, some call it the secret or hidden market. These are house sales that take place without a sign outside the property. There are lots of these; tapping into them is something I'll come back to later, but making contacts in the business is one of the keys to this.

I am not going to go into detail about how to renovate properties; there are entire TV series and many books dedicated to the subject. Very briefly, as you might expect from me by now, my main advice is to keep the costs down. I have seen lots of aspiring developers throw money away by decorating a property to their taste, only for the new owner to come in and undo all their work.

Make the property smart and clean, but enough of a blank canvas for someone to be able to stamp their own mark on the place. Keep that extra bit of profit for the next project.

LEASE OPTIONS

Lease options began life in the USA and have been going for about 10 years in the UK; with the economic downturn this route has been catching on more and more, and while it isn't a solution for everyone, it can work very well for the right person.

Who do lease options suit?
* People who can't get a 'traditional' mortgage
* People with no deposit
* People with bad credit history
* Potential landlords wanting to build a big property portfolio quickly
* People *needing* to sell, rather than *wanting* to sell

What is a lease options?
In a lease option, the property owner and investor can write an agreement in that, at the end of a specified rental or *lease* period (usually three or five years) the investor has the *option* of purchasing the property.

The option part of the agreement is literally that, and both parties can agree to prolong this period or re-negotiate at the end of the contracts period.

Where things can get a little complicated, and unlike traditional letting is that lease options allow for third parties to be involved. There can be a property owner, investor and a tenant buyer. So to keep things straight forward I am not going to get into too much detail here.

Example
For instance, a guy from the local neighbourhood came to see me a little while ago. Let's call him Mr Smith. He had run into financial difficulties and was struggling to pay his mortgage; another month or two down the line and he would be repossessed, losing everything.

I wouldn't do this for everyone, but in this case I bought the property and now rent it out to a third party. Mr Smith's house was worth £100,000 so I now pay the £450 per month mortgage. I rent it out for £700 per month, making a £250 a month profit.

In a couple of years, the new tenant buyer I found has the option of buying the property from me, getting it at the rate we agreed at the time of creating the lease.

The reason I use this example is that it demonstrates the importance of finding a **motivated seller.** A motivated seller is someone who needs to sell, and needs to sell quickly. Often sellers only have days left before a bank comes in repossesses their property. You can't get a quick sale through an estate agency as they just don't work that fast.

So, working with short time periods of weeks and days shows the importance of finding the right people who are suited for lease option deals.

Win-Win situation

On first thoughts you might think that to you are taking advantage of someone's unfortunate circumstances. In actual fact, you are helping that person as you are offering them a better deal than a bank. A bank would evict whoever was in the property and auction it for a great deal less than it was worth.

It is important to stress that someone in Mr Smiths position has nowhere to go for help. I was the only person that could help him at short notice. He didn't lose his house to the bank and suffer from the additional pain of having a bad credit score.

The benefit to me, as landlord, means I make some money on the rental income. I know that if I was faced with losing my property I would rather cut my losses and move on rather than lose everything for good. So it is a win-win.

Another scenario I have seen with lease options is when landlords have a difficult property on their books that they can't seem to let out: they can allow someone else to have a go by letting them have it on a lease option. This is a good option for people wanting to get a foothold in the property business and work up to the level of owning more properties on longer-term traditional mortgages.

There are lots of 'what if' scenarios with Lease Options and as it is a new area things are changing quickly. People are becoming more and more interested all the time so I am setting up seminars for people to find out more information.

The best thing to say at this time is that if Lease Options sound of interest to you and you want to find out more, get in touch (my details are in the back of the book) and I will do my best to help.

SHARED OWNERSHIP

In recent years I have seen a huge growth in shared ownership schemes. The 'shared' part of this is often members of the same family who help each other out, such as parents taking a part ownership in the house of one of their offspring.

They could pay the deposit for them, for example. Over a period of time, equity builds up in the property, and people move up the career ladder and earn more from their jobs. The mortgage holder can then buy the parent out of the property, and effectively, it is a leg-up on to the property ladder.

I have also been working increasingly with *property clubs,* which are based on a similar principle of shared ownership. They are usually a group of small investors, each with a sum they would like to put into a property. The club option allows people to minimise the risk of investing and also create collective bargaining power. The collective could all invest a sum for a property to be bought at auction, for example, and this would increase the likelihood for profit.

These property clubs are often made up of a collection of people from different backgrounds. They are not necessarily all experienced business people; some of the clubs I have worked with have involved 'second steppers' who want to invest a smallish sum of money.

BUY-TO-LET, A FIRST-TIMER'S GUIDE

This is the bread-and-butter of what a traditional landlord does, and it has become a huge area over the last few years. Below are a few tips which can save the first-time buy-to-let landlord a huge amount of aggravation.

The key issue for landlords is finding good, reliable tenants who

CASE STUDY – Buy-to-let

Mike and Maggie bought a buy-to-let property in the Easton area of Bristol at the end of the 1990s. The first thing Mike says is: 'It isn't money for old rope. Some people think landlords live the life of Riley, but we have had our fair share of stress and hassle.'

The instance he remembers most clearly was receiving a call one New Year's Day from their tenant who had returned home to find the front door kicked in. Mike remembers: 'We had to get something done about it there and then. It ended up costing us a fortune, but we had to act straight away.'

Having said that, the couple recognise that they have got a much better return on their investment than they would have if they had left their money in a bank. Over the 11 years they have been letting the property, the house has more than doubled in value. They say the modest yearly income from the rent doesn't quite break into the thousands, but a bank would have offered at best only a 6 per cent return on their money.

The couple are keen to stress that although they have done well on this investment, they have had to work for it. Another point Mike makes is that for the first few years they only broke even; it was only after the market improved that they started to see some equity develop.

His method of finding tenants is innovative: 'We offer the rent a bit below market value; what that does is create a lot of interest, and then we can pick and choose our tenants. We tend to go for younger couples in their twenties who you hope will look after the property and want to save some money. The other advantage of offering a slightly lower rent is that it means that tenants will usually stay for longer and you don't have all the hassle of finding new people again, and all the legwork that entails.'

Their strategy has worked well for them and they have no regrets. They even survived a landlord's worst nightmare, when someone used their property as a cannabis farm. This was discovered on one of their six-monthly check-ups of the property, they quickly dealt with the problem and the tenant was evicted.

There was some damage to the property and rent arrears were lost, but Mike is philosophical that it could have been a lot worse. 'There will always be people out there who see you as the enemy,' he says. 'Landlords are often as popular as traffic wardens. But if you treat people well and they treat you well in return, then it can be a very happy arrangement for all concerned.'

treat the property well, pay their rent on time and stay a reasonable length of time. This allows you to focus on other things rather than be constantly managing the property.

Where you find your tenants in the first place can influence the type you attract. Local websites, magazines and newspapers are all good, but I also think you can go a bit further and ask around; there is often a friend of a friend who is looking for somewhere to rent. I'd avoid renting a property to close friends, as there is always a possibility there could be some complications. Sometimes things can go wrong, or be slightly awkward, and it isn't worth falling out with good friends because of a dodgy boiler or because they fall behind in their rent.

When you have the tenant lined up, it is worth undertaking a few checks. People can be deceptive, and I have had very professional looking tenants who have left a place in a worse condition than others who might not look so smart.

SOME TIPS ON MANAGING PRIVATE RENTALS

Tenant Referencing

This is common practice these days, and you can do as much of it as you feel is necessary. A lot of this is covering your back against the worse-case scenario. As I have had practically every worse-case scenario happen to me over the years, I make sure that my property agency now does as much of the below as possible.

- **Photocopying ID documents** might help you if a tenant does a moonlight flit owing you lots of money (it can happen!).
- You can **credit check tenants,** which is cheap and easy to do online. Alternatively you can ask to see the last three months' banks statements, which is effectively doing your own credit check.
- You can ask for an **employer's reference** to check that tenants do exactly what they say they do. This sounds overly paranoid, but honestly, you would be amazed...
- Getting **references from past landlords** is also a common procedure these days, another way of making sure that a tenant doesn't have previous history of defaulting on payments. Just an email from the landlord is enough to put your mind at ease.
- If your tenants are young or cannot provide any of the above, you can ask for **guarantors**. A parent is the most common. Again, this is another way of covering your risk.
- **Next of kin** details can also mean you have an avenue to trace any tenants in that worse-case scenario.

More considerations with buy-to-let

Buy-to-let has had a lot of press over the past few years. For a while it was seen as a guaranteed way to make money, but nothing is ever really 100 per cent foolproof, as life and business just don't work that way.

I have read stories in the paper where people seem genuinely shocked to discover that someone might not automatically rent their property. A lot of this comes down to poor research, in my opinion. The above points into researching properties to flip equally apply to finding a buy-to-let, but there are other factors to consider, too.

Gardens are good for letting out for the family market, but will the tenant look after it? Employing someone to look after a garden is an additional drain on your profits.

Should you rent your property out as **unfurnished** or **furnished?** Furnished is good for younger tenants who might not have accumulated any furniture yet. That means it is good to make your property marketable, but on the other hand it is a cost, and means you need to think about an inventory. Deposits can be affected if things are damaged or broken during the term of a tenancy, and this can obviously be a source of dispute.

Unfurnished is much simpler; if the name of the game is ultimately to let the property tick over by itself, then the less you have to manage the better. But if you are making it difficult to let because the market is demanding something else, then perhaps you need to think again.

The Golden Rules of making money from rented property are essentially to make sure you are buying in an area that has a strong demand for such properties. Over and above that, you must safeguard your investment by taking the precautions outlined above on your tenant's ability to pay the rent.

Despite the recession, the buy-to-let market is still very buoyant. In fact it is *because of the recession*, as many people are choosing to rent rather than buy while the global markets are so shaky, or they cannot buy because the banks are not lending money as freely as they were five years ago. Yet there are still 'buy-to-let' mortgages available if you have some equity in your own to use as leverage.

The signs at the time of going to press are very encouraging, but as with all of this we have to exercise some caution and do our research.

To manage or not to manage?

You have a choice with buy-to-let whether to manage the property yourself or to bring in a company to do the day-to-day stuff.

Which is going to work for you? This largely depends on you. If you think you can manage with someone calling you first thing in the morning to tell you their boiler has broken, then good for you. Do it, don't pay a property management company to do it for you and charge you for the priviledge.

On the other hand, if you want to leave the donkey work to someone else while you are getting on with the important things in life – maybe enjoying your retirement – then go for it.

Try and get a recommendation if you can, and if you can't, then try finding a local company that is hungry for the business. You need a company that will act and get things done for you and your tenants. If it leaves them waiting, this can reflect very badly on you and mean a faster turnover of tenants – and as I have said before, this eats into your profit.

SOCIAL HOUSING

Many people shy away from dealing with social housing as it means dealing with local councils and tenants who are claiming benefits.

But I feel there are many plus points to letting out to social tenants. Once all the paperwork is sorted there is a steady income, and benefit tenants are much more likely to stay for a longer period, as they don't relish going through all the hassle with the council again. I see it is as a win-win.

Besides, you are helping out people, and as much as I like making money I also like to help out people – as long as it still makes money in the long term, which it does. Who says landlords can't have a social conscience?

HMOS

The clearest benefit of houses of multiple occupancy is that you can make more profit from four or five people than you can from one or two. Downsides? There is often more work involved in managing the property as you are increasing the chances of tenant turnover and all the paperwork that creates. There is also the added wear and tear pressure on the house and its contents.

But if you can deal with these issues – and, of course, the market place within which you are working can sustain a flow of tenants – then the financial rewards make it worthwhile.

The trick with HMOs is often in filling your houses, of which some people are now specialising, including a colleague of mine working in Bristol. Here Taylor explains a bit more about her strategy.

WHAT TYPE OF INVESTOR ARE YOU?

THE FIRST TIME INVESTOR'

As with Taylor's example, it is good to devise your own strategy. Everybody has to start somewhere; for most people the only investments they will ever make are in their own houses, and maybe a pension.

But once you have made one investment, why stop there? For most of us it is going to take 25 years of going to work every day to pay off the mortgage – a never-ending cycle of work, work, work.

If I told you you could work for yourself, be your own boss, and most importantly stop when you want to because you have made enough money, I am sure most people would see the attraction in that.

On any journey the first step is the hardest to take, so if you are convinced and ready to set off, the first thing you need to do it assess what you have that you could use to buy your first property.

NO MONEY, NO EXCUSE!

One of the first rules of business is that you need money to make money, but most people are scared of asking for help when it comes to money. In my experience there is always money somewhere. See the **raising finance** section later in this chapter for some tips and advice on this.

THE SECOND STEPPER

This is the person who has done the above, built a bit of equity and is ready to make the next move. Some property experts claim you can achieve the goal of making enough income to live on from four properties (including the one you live in).

You will also see a lot of talk in property books about what they call creating a **passive income**. This is essentially making money from rental properties while you sleep. Employ a property management company to look after your properties, and you would never even have to get out of bed!

This is a good target to have early on, though only you will know how far the limit is. I have gone into hundreds of properties, but as you will know by now I set my targets high. I hope you are at the least looking to make a good living from this; you need to work out what a 'good living' means to you and work those figures into your business plan and strategy.

One word of advice for any new investor is not to get accustomed to low interest rates. Although the outlook looks good on that front for the foreseeable future, this isn't something you can assume is here to stay. Try to build a bit of leeway into your plans and projections to counter any future changes to interest rates.

A SILENT INVESTOR

This is the ideal strategy for someone who has money to invest

CASE STUDY – Houses of multiple occupancy

Taylor has only been working in the property business for a year, so she is an interesting person to speak to for several reasons. She started working in the current recession and has gone about building her business in entirely the correct way. She has built a strategy which includes using lease options and letting HMO properties. Using lease options means she has been able to start working in property without taking out a mortgage, and I was interested to hear her views on this.

You have built a property business without taking out a mortgage. Can you explain a bit more about this?
I had no credit history as I was not born in England, so I have had to think of how to work around this. Basically, I take difficult-to-let properties and make myself the go-between, finding the tenants and doing the work required to make the property rentable.

I take out a lease option with the landlord, meaning they make enough to cover their mortgage on the property and I make my profit on the difference. It is a win-win situation. The landlord is no longer losing money, and I am making a profit. And the house is no longer empty, which is good for the neighbourhood.

Where do you find your properties?
I find most of them through estate agents; they are usually from landlords who have had trouble letting them themselves. They are usually happy to get the property off their books, as it has become a liability to them.

Do the properties require work?

Usually just cosmetic stuff. Typically, I'll put about £3,000 into a property to make it HMO standard. HMO houses have strict regulations such as fire doors and the like. You also have to think that the shared spaces are going to get worked quite hard, so I look for hard-wearing products to save replacing them again in another year's time.

What advice do you have for people thinking of moving into letting property?

Stick to one strategy and hang on tight to your plan. Find an idea which works best for you, in your area. You have to think hard about both of these elements. Also ask 'where are my tenants going to come from?' I have focused on one plan, on one area. Later, I will look to do other things, such as getting mortgages, but first of all I have to get this to work.

And is it working?

I think the proof is in the figures. I didn't earn anything for the first six months, but since then I have been clearing £5,000 profit per month. I am saving as much as possible to improve my credit score so I can make further investments in the future and eventually become a landlord in the more traditional sense.

but wants to have less involvement in the day-to-day business of managing properties and tenants and all the headaches they can bring.

Silent investment can be on a short-term or long-term basis, whichever the investor prefers. Short-term in property terms usually means a couple of months in order to flip a property. There are never any guarantees that you will make your money back, but if you do your research, work with people who know what they are doing and invest wisely, then the rewards can be good for minimal effort. Essentially, you are just letting your money do the work.

Longer-term investments can mean leaving your money in a property and letting it grow over the years.

An advantage of being an investor generally is that you can choose whether you get involved on a deal-by-deal basis. In an ideal world it is best to have a number of investments on the go, a mixture of short- and long-term.

This means you are not in a position where you are waiting for one project to pay the dividends in order to move on to your next one – a frustrating situation to be in.

JOINT VENTURES

Joint ventures have all the advantages of the above but you also have the added security of investing with others, reducing your own exposure to risk. Of course, it also means you have to share the spoils.

Another advantage is that in working with other investors, hopefully you will have the opportunity to work with them again. Learn from them, pick up tips and gain from their experience.

MAKING YOUR FIRST PROPERTY DEAL

OK, we have had a look at the different types of property investment and the different types of property investors who are out there.

Now you know all this background stuff you can get into the exciting bit.

Your first deal is often the hardest one. Remember that you are on a learning curve. Once you have got familiar with all the steps you need to take, it will be much easier to repeat next time.

STEP 1 - CREATE YOUR TEAM

Before you rush down to the estate agents and start browsing properties (the fun part), make sure you have made contact with the people who will help you through:

- Mortgage broker/finance
- Solicitor
- Conveyancer (easiest way of finding these is recommendation from your estate agent)

If you are going to flip the property, you will also need to have tradesmen you trust to work with. These guys are a vital cog; without knowing if you have someone to do the work, how can you create a credible business plan for your first deal?

The process of selling is usually looked after by the estate agent. However it is important to know how it works, and the steps are generally as follows:

1	Raising finance
2	Find property
3	Instruct your solicitor
4	Make an offer
5	Offer agreed
6	Conveyancing
7	Survey
8	Accept mortgage offer
9	Exchange contracts
10	Completion

Let's take look at some of these in a little more detail:

STEP 2 - RAISE FINANCE

As I said earlier, one of the most common excuses people find for **not investing** is: *I can't afford it.*

But let's think about this a bit more. Chances are the reason you are reading this book is because you want to do something to change your circumstances. Investing in property is about creating another source of income, which will add to or replace your wage and hopefully your pension as well. So the real question is: *Can you afford not to?*

In my experience, there is always money somewhere. If you don't have it yourself directly to hand, it doesn't mean you can't make your deal. The first thing you need to do is to change your thinking. As I had to myself.

Most of us are told debt is bad. Debt *is* bad if you can't pay it back, and it gets out of control. But as long as you are sensible and do your maths – and you do your research into the market so you are taking a calculated risk – then a short-term debt will get you on the road to long-term financial stability.

There are also lots of sources of finance, including:

- Credit cards
- Loans
- Overdrafts
- Private investors
- Inheritance
- Family and friends

Have you checked all these off to make sure you have left no stone unturned?

Is there equity in the family?

This doesn't necessarily involve calling up that long-lost uncle and asking to borrow enough money to cover a deposit (although it could be if you were happy to do this). A more likely scenario is getting the assistance from an older generation of your family who have paid off their mortgage or have built up equity. They might be able to help you by acting as a **mortgage guarantor**. This scenario is becoming much more common as first-time buyers are struggling to get the access to the finance that was more easily available a few years ago

Another situation I have seen is when parents have signed over their house to their children as an early **inheritance**. This is becoming more common as it is a way of avoiding inheritance tax, which currently stands at a whopping 40 per cent. The inheritance tax threshold for 2012-13 is £325,000.

What about credit cards?

A lot of people will tell you to avoid credit card debt like the plague. As I mentioned above, I have discovered that there are **good debts** and **bad debts**.

Good debt is when you are using the money to create money. A mortgage is a loan, most of us have one, and people can generally see this type of loan as worth the risk over the long term.

Used in the right way, a credit card debt can act positively. The aim is to get you up a rung on the property ladder which in turn creates a greater level of **financial leverage** in the future. Financial leverage is basically having the equity in a property to be able to use it for a future investment.

So you need to be wise about what you are using the debt for. Bad debt is using finance to buy stuff that won't appreciate in value – clothes, eating out, going on holiday.

Hopefully, you will need to use some of these techniques only for the first transaction, but what I really aim to achieve here is the change your attitude from 'I can't...' to 'I could if I did X, Y and then Z!'

Do you really need all that stuff?

People sometime laugh at me when I ask them if they have anything they can sell. But seriously, are you driving an expensive car? A car will only depreciate in value; property can go up and make you money – and it is for the long term. Sell the car, sell the designer clothes on eBay, sell those collectable things you have been saving for a rainy day. This is that rainy day!

I worked with someone who was trying to raise as much finance as possible and he did all of the above, sold all his designer stuff and downgraded his car, and came back with £15,000. This took him more than half way to his target for a deposit.

Different people have different ideas of what stuff they need in their life. If you can cut back and create some cash that can be used for a project, then this is putting your assets to much better use than stuff that is just taking up space in your house.

Can you find a private investor?

As the recession bites, people with money are looking to spread their risks. There are professional investors out there who might be interested in having a stake in your enterprise. Have a look around, speak to some people and see if you can find them.

There are usually investors' clubs. They may not be advertised widely, but get into some business networks and you will soon work out where they are. I am using private investors more and more as I am finding the banks are becoming difficult to deal with.

Another option is to come back to friends and family. That rich uncle, chances are he might know a thing or two about money. Maybe he would be interested in investing with you?

If you have spotted a property that would be great for a buy-to-let, for example, but you don't have the finance to get you the mortgage, it is better to take a bit of a loss on the profit by working with someone than not take the opportunity at all. Once you have repaid the investor, you can go on to make other deals which are all yours. Think about the long term.

Pensions

You cannot transfer any money that you have accumulated in a pension into a mortgage, but if you are approaching pensionable age and expecting a lump sum, then this could be the springboard you need to get your project up and running.

A lump sum sitting in the bank is only ever going to pay you a certain level of interest – but by investing it in the right project means you can continue to generate an income, even though your working days are behind you.

What is next?

You have decided what kind of investment and strategy suits you. You have worked out where the money is going to come from. Next it is time to get down to the serious business of finding that property.

STEP 3 – FIND A PROPERTY

The next part of the puzzle is finding the ideal property – and here I am going to give you the benefit of my years of experience.

Finding 'below the market value' properties

As I mentioned earlier, to maximize your profit on either flipping a property or on letting it out you need to be get it for under the market value. Here are some ways to find such properties:

Leafletting

You have probably seen a leaflet come through your front door asking if you are considering selling. Leafleting is cheap and also allows you to target specific areas or streets you know fit the bill of what you are looking for. You can design the leaflet on your home computer and get it printed at a local print shop. There are companies out there that will deliver leaflets for you, you can pay someone you know to do it, or you can do it yourself and save yourself some money.

Social media

Social media are becoming more and more prevalent in life and business. Facebook and Twitter can be great sources of networking and business opportunities, but a word of caution is to be careful not to upset or alienate your followers. Sometimes business and your personal life are best kept separate. I keep my personal life on Facebook and use Twitter for business.

Another thing it took me a while to realise with Twitter is that it has its own etiquette. It is actually much more effective to engage your followers on business generally and then do a bit of self promotion. I have seen other users get on people's nerves by promoting themselves all the time and not giving any attention to others who are doing interesting things. These people generally lose followers rather than attract them.

Remember what I said earlier about the kinds of reasons people might want to sell their houses quickly. They may not be the kind of people who are on the look-out for a buyer or have their houses on the open market, so essentially these tools are ways of reaching out to them and **tapping into the 'hidden market'.**

Advertising

I have seen **advertising** signs up on busy roads, which is a bit 'in your face' but I am sure it works and has the desired effect. Almost certainly contravening local byelaws, too – but there are also cards in shop windows and classified advertising columns in local newspapers which are both legal and relatively cheap.

There is a lot of advertising that you can pay for on the internet, which has much lower overheads as you only pay if customers click through. This is how Google Ads works: you pay them every time someone clicks through from an affiliate site, but your ads will come up only on websites that are relevant to your services.

Word of mouth

In addition to advertising you also need to 'put the word out', let your friends and family know what you are up to. It is important to keep the message simple. Think of Chinese Whispers and how easy it is for people to get the wrong end of the stick. So 'I am looking for a house in this area' is easier for people to pass on than 'I am looking for a classic period property in any of the following areas, with a view to either investing long-term as a buy-to-rent or perhaps as a multiple-occupancy let'. Make it easy enough for your great-grandmother to pass the word on.

If you have built up contacts in the property business, call on them and ask if they know of any properties the vendor might let go for under the market value. It is not uncommon for landlords to want to let a property go quickly. They might need the ready cash to invest in another project, perhaps that property has been difficult to let for some reason – check why, of course – or maybe they just feel as if they have too much to manage. Whatever the reason, a good estate agent will see the benefit in helping a client and hooking them up with the budding entrepreneur that is you.

STEP 4 – THE PROCESS OF SELLING A HOUSE

Selling properties is at the heart of the business. Everything else is irrelevant if there isn't the sale in the first place to build upon.

This is a **step-by-step guide** on the sales process. Tips on *how* to sell the house are in the next section.

1 An **Energy Performance Certificate** (EPC) is a legal requirement, and you will need to have applied for this before you market your property. The EPC doesn't need to have arrived for the sale to go through, although you must have commissioned one. An EPC gives information on how to make your home more energy efficient and reduce carbon dioxide emissions. All homes bought, sold or rented now require an EPC.

You can find someone to come and do an EPC for you locally

(internet, Yellow Pages or estate agent) and give you the certificate for anything between £35 to £50.

2 Photographs are hugely important nowadays. The internet is the first place most people start looking now, so you need to make a good early impression. You can take photos of your property with a digital camera and upload them to a website.

You then add details about your home, taking time to make sure you word the **description** in an appealing manner. It may be worth it in the long run to pay someone to take photos for you. You can do exactly the same thing with the floor plan, which is another small job.

3 The good old fashioned **advertising sign** outside the house has been proved to help substantially with the marketing of a property.

4 Arranging viewings is something you can do yourself if you are selling privately, or let the agent take care of.

5 Contact your solicitor and let them know you would like to get paperwork in order in preparation for a buyer. If you do not have a solicitor, I suggest you ask family and friends for a recommendation. Good solicitors are worth their weight in gold, so get a recommendation and don't scrimp on this.

6 You should receive a **fixtures and fittings** form and a preliminary enquiries form to fill in from your solicitor. Get these completed and sent back as soon as you can, as there might be extra paperwork that needs hunting down, such as planning permissions, building regulation approval or details of your lease.

7 Negotiating the selling price is the exciting part: a potential purchaser will make you an offer through your agent or direct, and you decide whether to accept it or hold out for something better.

8 Next, you **exchange contracts** and swap solicitors' details to create a completion date. You then need to instruct your solicitor, giving them all the details of the buyer and sale.

9 To reach **completion** you need to vacate the property if you are in it. The money from the buyer is sent to your solicitor, who will pay any charges against the property, principally your mortgage and generally their fees. The remaining money will either be used to buy your next home or sent to you directly.

This is how the sales process works on paper. I should add that I have spent many a long hour chasing up solicitors and waiting for mortgages to come through. Numerous things can come along to slow or complicate the process, but nine times out ten all goes according to plan.

THE BUSINESS
OF PROPERTY

PART
4

I love business. For me there is nothing greater than the buzz of making a deal. Think for a second: everything around us involves the world of business – and it is nothing to be frightened of. If we educate ourselves about how business works, we are educating ourselves about how the world works. I would say that I feel more empowered than ever. When I was a younger man and just out of school, I had no clue as to what made everything tick.

Over the years I have learned a lot. But there is always more to learn, and the world changes, so I encourage you to do what I do, which is keep reading and talking to people and never falling into the trap of thinking you know it all. I didn't do well in school or go to university. I think self-education is the key, taking control for yourself. There are lots of great teachers out there, and many of them have written great books or put themselves on You Tube.

'Deal or no Deal'

In this section I will set out more key things I have learned about the property business. Much of this information will apply to any business. I talk a lot about 'making deals', and while I am referring to buying and selling houses, you could equally apply this knowledge to selling baked beans.

In this section I will look at:
- Top 10 selling tips
- Adding Value to Property
- Keeping an eye on the bottom line
- Organic Growth
- People Skills
- Listening to criticism

TOP 10 SELLING TIPS

Markets are obviously going to be different in different areas of the country, but these tips have always worked for me in Bristol. One important tip is to view the property as just that, no more. 'A property' might be your home but when it is on the market you have to see it simply as a business commodity.

Get your timing right
Spring and summer are peak selling periods in many markets, not just property. Thankfully, this is also when most properties look their best. Late summer and when the school year starts tend to be slow times, as do Christmas and the first months of the New Year.

Create kerb appeal
Before making an appointment to view, most potential buyers will check out your property from the road. It is important to create a good first impression, and most potential buyers will be looking to see if they need to spend much money on the property. Any junk lying around that looks as if it has been there a long time, or overgrown weeds, can send a message that the house has not been particularly well maintained.

A fresh lick of paint and tidying the garden can be all it needs to create a good impression.

Light and bright
A bit of emulsion can be the best investment you make. I am sure you have heard this before, but keep it neutral and clean. It is the blank canvas approach you want to create, so potential buyers feel like they can add their own mark on the property when they move in.

Clutter Free
Space is very attractive to any potential buyer, so create the illusion of it by clearing your stuff away for viewings. Get it into the attic, or

into storage. Buyers want to be able to visualise all their belongings in the house, and this is much easier to do when there isn't someone else's stuff competing for their attention.

Dress to impress

This is about trying to make the house as attractive as possible. Reinstalling some original features, having nice doors or nice floors can really clinch the sale if your buyers have the option of a couple of houses which are vying for their attention.

Updating the curtains or replacing a bit of tatty carpet can make a huge difference. Other considerations are to have subtle lighting and avoid strong smells in the house.

Keep it clean

OK, this is obvious, but I have looked at lots of houses over the years and you would be amazed at the lack of effort that some people make. It also reassures buyers that the whole house has been maintained, not just the surface stuff.

Kitchen matters

Kitchens and bathrooms are the two areas that cost the most in a house. No wonder these are crucial areas for potential buyers. If the house you are selling has a kitchen that looks a little tired, give it a boost by adding new doors, handles or worktops.

It may even pay to replace it: the cost of putting in a new kitchen can outweigh the cost of having the property sitting on the market for months waiting for a purchaser.

Bathroom basics

At the moment the trend is most definitely for white bathrooms, and it has been for years. Anything else is a 1970s throwback and dates the property considerably. – to the extent where an apricot bath suite could lose you a potential sale. Cleanliness, lightness and freshness are the keys for a decent bathroom.

The outdoor life

You don't have to create an urban oasis to sell your house, but a tidy and well maintained garden creates a very good impression, particularly for families. If your fingers aren't particularly green, get a local gardener in.

People skills

The next part of this chapter is all about people skills, but this is a good example of why people skills are so important. When meeting any potential buyers, you want to be exude an air of confidence while remaining approachable. You can provide good local knowledge of the area and the property itself; be on hand, but don't follow people around the house.

ADDING VALUE TO PROPERTY

- **Converting your loft** can add up to 20 per cent to the price of your property – but not every home is suited to a loft conversion. Thirties semis and Victorian properties are among those that can work well. A good rule of thumb is to see how many other properties on the street have already done the same. A quick 'Velux check' might tell you whether it is worth the investment.

- **Adding an extension** can also add value, if it is properly executed and appropriate to the house. Avoid upsetting the neighbours.

- **Building a garage** if you have the space free on the property and it is in an urban area. Getting the planning permission might be enough to add some value, but be careful not to go the other way and turn a garage into a room, since this very often doesn't add value.

- **Adding a bathroom** can be very appealing, particularly to families with teenage children. You have to weigh up whether it will pay to have a bigger bathroom rather than an extra bedroom, but in some cases it can. Definitely worth looking in to.

- **Updating the kitchen and bathroom,** as mentioned above.

- **Installing central heating** if there isn't any in the house, as this is a big, disruptive job that can be very off-putting to people who only want to make cosmetic improvements.

- **Fitting double glazing** is a great way of keeping heat in and noise out. It also helps reduce bills.

- **Obtaining planning permission** can sometimes be enough for someone who doesn't want the hassle of living through the disruption of that kitchen extension or new garage.

My final piece of advice when it comes to selling a property or adding value to property links us nicely with the next part of this chapter. It is easy when sprucing up a house to spend too much money. Keep an eye on this – it is 'sprucing-up', not renovating. Those two things are very different, and can spell the difference between success and failure.

BUYING AT AUCTION

Buying a house at auction differs from buying property on the open market, in so much as when the auctioneer's gavel comes down, the deal is final – and the cost of the property must be paid in full although now some auctions do offer you 30 days to get your finance together.

This is why auctioned properties are cheaper; this and the fact that although you can often view the property, you don't have the added security of getting it checked out by your own surveyors. Auctions provide bargains, but they can also turn into real cans of worms.

KEEPING AN EYE ON THE BOTTOM LINE

I have an accountant and a book-keeper, and even though I trust both of them to do their jobs I check the balance sheet and the bank accounts daily. When I do this, I am taking the temperature of the business. I am checking to see if the books are healthy, whether cash-flow is healthy and if anyone owes the business money.

I am not being a control freak, but I can only sleep soundly if I know that everything is ticking along nicely. If a train is coming, I want to know that, and be prepared for it!

Ultimately you are only successful in business if you manage to stay in business, and if you are working on a shoestring then you need to keep an eye on every penny.

Example: Over-confidence

A guy I know who moved into property during the boom years had a tactic which always had me worried. He never held any equity in any of his properties, which was fine while prices were rising during the noughties. I would try to encourage him to exercise some caution, because we never know when the markets are going to change, but his attitude was very gung-ho, as if he were untouchable. As much as I admire confidence, equally I think that part of the trick is knowing when to be gung-ho and when to exercise caution.

Keeping an eye on the bottom line isn't just about making sure you are in profit in the short term. In an ideal world you also need to make sure you have a buffer zone or a cushion to protect you from the unknown – unexpected costs, or a reduction in the property market. This is being prepared for the long-term.

ORGANIC GROWTH

I am a firm believer in organic growth. Growth does not happen overnight, it is something that is nurtured and harvested. Whatever the size of the business, and whatever the business, take it one step at a time, while always keeping that vision in your mind of how you ultimately want the business to look.

PEOPLE SKILLS

Ultimately, all business is about people, and some people are naturally blessed with people skills. Others have to work a bit harder at it. Whichever you are, I think it is worth knowing a bit about these techniques.

How do you build rapport?

Building rapport is the essence of people skills. The best business people make this appear effortless, and I am lucky enough to have worked with some amazing people who are naturals at it. They like people, and people like them. Think of Richard Branson: he is a likable guy who you can imagine would be really entertaining if you were to get stuck in a lift with him.

Like any skill, you can improve your ability to build rapport with people, even if you are not a natural. I did this by watching some great sales people and seeing what they did.

Mirroring is a well known, tried and tested 'trick' of sales people who replicate the body language of their clients. This is something to be aware of but could be a bit transparent, so use it with caution.

Humour can break down barriers like nothing else. If it is natural to you, use it intelligently rather than coming across as a joker.

Common interests obviously bond people, so to build rapport find areas of common ground. Think of those cheesy American sales people you see on TV asking about the kids: this is exactly what they are doing. Obviously I don't expect you to be this cheesy, but it proves the point – the kinds of banter I overhear are typically based around shared experiences such as football or even *The X Factor.*

Don't over do it

Another danger zone I have noticed with rapport is best illustrated by sales people who have a reputation for having 'the gift of the gab'. As much as I have seen great sales people exploit this ability, I have seen just as many talk themselves *in* and then *out* of the sale. Knowing when to talk and when to shut up is a great skill. It also comes with confidence. Sales people will often chatter on much longer than they need to, maybe to cover their own nervous excitement at having made a sale. Relax, the sale is made. By all means continue with some chit-chat about the weather if needs be, but be careful not to let your guard down and let the customer slip through your fingers after you have put in all that work.

Example: Poor people skills, poor business.

I had an old friend get in touch and ask me for some help in getting a few properties. No problem, I gave him the number of a good agent. I then gave him the numbers of some of my trusted team members – builders, plumbers. I even gave him the number for my solicitor. I basically gave him everything on a plate.

A couple of months later I started getting phone calls from my old friend, basically berating the builders and plumbers who had walked out of the job. I didn't want to get involved, but these were also guys who worked for me, so I wanted to make sure they weren't going to hold it against me!

The word came back that my old friend gave the guys very little direction in what he wanted from them. He basically gave them the keys to the properties and left them to get on with it.

He started paying them weekly, which they liked. But then he changed to paying them monthly as he started going over his budget, without telling them he was doing so. Understandably, they were livid when they weren't paid as usual, and started to fear the worst.

I was surprised to hear that my old friend was so poor at this, as I knew he had been a manager before. If he had laid out at the beginning what he expected, how he was going to pay, when the work should be completed and agree how much it was going to cost, then all that bother could have been avoided.

Build rapport with your team, keep talking, and manage the situation before it turns around and starts managing you!

Handling objections

All sales and business negotiations will involve handling objections. An objection is the very normal response that stands between us and making the deal. If someone offers me a 'bargain', I am usually very suspicious and my objections are often questions to find out more about this opportunity.

Estate agents are a key part of the buying and selling process, and their wage will often depend on the commission they can make from selling houses. Naturally, they will be working hard to make the sale and thinking of how to overcome your objections. A good example of this is **estate agent-speak,** designed to counter your objections.

Buyer	Estate Agent
The garden is too small	It is well appointed
It is on a main road	Close to transport links
In the middle of nowhere	In a secluded location
A bit of an odd layout	This charming property…

This is a humorous example, but what I am trying to get across is that objections are often necessary discussions we need to have to see things differently. What the estate agent is essentially saying is: 'OK. It isn't perfect, but what else are you going to get with your budget? Get real.' They are using their people skills to subtly change your mind.

Lots of people new to business tend to take it for granted that No means No. It doesn't always, so listen to the objection and learn to counter it.

Think of it like a game of tennis:

You serve: It's £150,000
They return: Too much
You return: OK, I'll give you a 10 per cent discount
They return: 15 per cent
Your return: OK, let's settle for 12.5 per cent

This haggling process goes back a long way, and nine times out of ten the deal gets done in the three steps. You have taken the sale from negotiations right up to the final part, where you are ready to close. The close is your unreturnable forehand smash!

Closing the deal

This is the part when the salesperson has said all they have to say. The customer is showing all the signs that the sale is made, but you just need to finish it off. Time to seal the deal.

Often the job is done, and you just need to sweat out those final few seconds while the customer fully makes their mind up.

The 'silent close' is an old sales trick, employed once you have said your piece. The customer is mulling over the final few points in their mind, but instead of talking more and giving the customer the opportunity to slip away, you back them into a position where it is crunch time. Yes or no? Deal or no deal?

The silence comes in because we all find silences awkward. Faced with silence there is always going to be the temptation to fill that silence.

Hold your nerve, let the customer fill that silence, and get ready to shake hands to confirm the deal!

Taking the knocks of 'business life'

When business is on a roll, there is nothing better than being in business. But equally you need to be able to deal with the tough times, in fact this might be the most important lessons of all.

You win some and you lose some

You won't make every deal. People are unpredictable and you don't always know why someone says no. You could be selling something that saves or makes someone money, and they will still say no. This is just a fact of life, and there will be occasions when you need to let go and move on to the next deal.

Knock on enough doors and one will open

There will be days when it seems that you are flogging a dead horse, and nobody is interested in what you have to have offer – however good the deal is. There is nothing you can do but keep a positive attitude and keep going. I have seen business people get really down in the dumps when their business slows down, and this can create a self-fulfilling prophesy.

No deal = depressed business person = no sales.

But keep going, stay positive and try and break this circle. There is always light at the end of the tunnel and one of the biggest lessons in any kind of business is just to tough it out. You may go through a process of questioning everything and reappraising what you have to offer, but ultimately you just have to keep the faith and go for it.

Sometimes the harder you try, the harder it becomes

Sometimes when times get tough people can oversell their products. We all have experience of pushy salespeople, and nobody likes to be bullied into buying something. Pull back, relax, keep promoting the positive elements of whatever your product is and the sales will come. Desperation is a big turn-off; never appear desperate (even if you are!)

Dealing with droughts
Every seasoned business person will experience a lean time when nothing seems to go their way. There is nothing to do but plough on, it is back to the numbers game. All droughts end eventually.

A cautionary note on dealing with banks

Up until now I have talked about property as a great vehicle for building a business and making a good living. Of course you don't need me to tell you that all business comes with a risk, but there are other sharks in the water you need to watch out for. They appear friendly at first, they court your business and offer to help you out. But these friendly creatures can turn into foes in a very quick time, and their bite is definitely as bad as their bark!

I am talking about banks.
With the recession of the last few years I and many people working in property have been getting a hard time from some banks, the same banks that previously couldn't do enough to help us. Now they want to reduce our overdraft limits and they have devalued properties, ignoring our protests that they are misguided in their calculations.

This has been a big shock to me, but it has also given me a reality check. I am now doing what I have been advising in this chapter. I am looking for money from investors, I am looking to go into ventures with friends, I am setting up property clubs. The banks can't necessarily be relied on, as they can pull the rug from under you when they so choose.

I should point out I am not talking about every single bank here.

It is my main bank that hasn't helped me the most. What I have discovered is that there are other banks out there that are still being reasonable and willing to lend, so I am moving my business to the people who want that business and are willing to treat my profession with a bit more respect.

I am also not putting all my eggs in one basket. I am spreading the money around as much as possible – with regards to investment and where I look for credit.

My tip is to have a few bank accounts for your business transactions. I have, and while some banks are reining in, I am relying on the one that is still lending. This means I can keep my business on track.

MANAGEMENT SKILLS
Learning how to lead

Being your own boss is great,
no-one tells you what to do,
you call the shots.

Being your own boss is a nightmare,
no-one tells you what to do,
you call the shots.

These two statements reveal the double-edged sword that is being your own boss. Ultimately, the buck stops with me. And if you go into business, the buck will stop with you.

We get used to letting people tell us what to do. Our parents tell us what to do. Then school tells us what to do. Then we go to work and our boss tells us what to do. Anyone who has children will recognise that unfortunately you have to rein in kids a lot. This isn't a bad thing. It is a fact of life. The tricky bit comes when we want to make something happen for ourselves. Let's face it, unless we are extremely lucky, nobody else is going to come along with a magic wand and transform our lives for us.

So let's get on with it. How do we become a leader?

That doesn't mean you have to start bossing everyone around and becoming a real pain in the neck. The best leaders **lead by example**. They know what they want to achieve and they set about making it happen, usually one step at a time.

One of the key assets for any leader is the ability to listen – not just to your staff but to your market and the team you build around you. Market conditions change all the time, and you need to keep one step ahead of the game. Be aware of new trends, talk to people who work in different areas of your sector to find out what they are experiencing.

Motivating others

Human beings are one of the most unpredictable animals on the planet – and working in any business means working with other people. Getting the best out of people around you is always hard. If you are employing them full-time or just on a contract basis to complete one job, you want to make sure you are getting the best for your money.

I find one of the key tactics is to treat people as you would like to be treated yourself. If we remain professional, courteous and business-like, hopefully – I say hopefully as we can't always predict this – those around us will do the same.

People are different from one another, of course and it is worth spending the time with your staff to find out what motivates them. Maybe they are working their way up the career ladder, or maybe it is money that drives them.

Someone once told me that what motivates most of us is recognition. Having a boss who acknowledges the work we have put in and spends the time with us to discuss it is one of the simplest and easiest way to keep people motivated.

I make sure I always spend a bit of time catching up with staff, usually one to one and away from their desk. This small 'time-out' is usually all it takes to discover any looming issues, and prevents small aggravations becoming anything more serious. People can build up resentments that aren't necessarily your fault, but as 'the boss' it is likely that you might have to take the flak.

The lesson: Prevent your staff from building up any resentment or becoming demotivated by always making sure you have time for them and thanking them for their work.

I like to give praise for a job **well done** – and it is always well received, because I do not give praise easily.

I also **set targets** for myself and my staff. I think we have a natural tendency to underestimate ourselves, and setting the bar high brings out the best in us.

Delegation

When you start running your own business the temptation is to do everything yourself, feeling the more you do the more you keep costs down. But you are only human, and the truth is that sometimes we make better business decisions if we are little bit removed from things and have the space to think.

The key to allowing yourself more time and space is to delegate tasks, even if they are things you could do yourself. This is part of time management, which I talk more of below.

It is why a lot of businessmen go out and play golf. They are networking, plus they are creating space and time to think about 'the big stuff'. Developing the strategy for the business, new lines of income, new products, better ways of doing things…

I also think that it is a false economy to try and do everything yourself. That way, you can do the job but you can't get the volume done, and this is a key lesson in business. You may have discovered a way to make a few pounds, but creating volume – *ie* more turnover – in your business will make all the difference with your bottom line.

Initially there is a transition period, as the profit you were once making suddenly disappears into the new member of staff. But keep working, manage your members of staff and they will push you – and the profits – up to a new plateau.

Once things settle down and your team has picked up doing all the work you used to do yourself, you can then look at **diversifying**.

Diversifying

I won't say too much about this now, as I have written this section of the book for people starting out in business. But it is worth understanding why businesses diversify. Essentially, diversifying is good business, and means you can respond to the changing nature of the market.

No business is ever immune to up and downs, and diversification means that another line in the business can keep the cash flow steady. It is also easier to make additional deals with your business contacts than it is to go and find new contacts.

This is also known as 'selling-up', and fast food restaurants are masters at this. You go in for a burger, but you end up buying the meal because they make it better value.

Or take your insurance company: you want car insurance but they offer breakdown cover and household insurance as well, and you end up with all three.

If you are starting out, you may not have thought this far ahead, but don't worry at this stage. If you have spotted various potential opportunities for your enterprise, you have to decide whether to launch one or all at the same time. The business itself will often influence this decision.

My diversifications have been quite different, and provide me with contrasting challenges. That is what I like. I like to be kept on my toes!

Strategic partnerships/building a good team

You cannot succeed alone in business. As much as a business person needs to be able to be a bit of an all-rounder, people have different strengths and it always pays to get a specialist team around you.

Your own team needs to be comprised of people who you can

work with and people who can work with you. But you also need to build a good relationship with the people you just come into day-to-day contact with. Look after them, and they will look after you.

Don't assume that 'building a team' around you means a huge outlay of money, I am not necessarily suggesting taking on people as permanent staff to achieve this. I work with many people who are paid on an 'as and when' basis.

In my line of business I need builders, mortgage providers, estate agents and others. These are my team: they need me and I need them. That is why you have to work hard to make sure that they like working with you and think of you before they think of one of your competitors. At the end of the day, **people buy into people**.

With the permanent staff I now have running my lettings agency I like to have regular meetings so we are all clear and on what needs to be done and by when. This applies to me, as well as them.

Time management

All the above planning and organisation can go to waste if we don't manage our time effectively.

Some statistics suggest that poor time management wastes the UK up £80bn a year, which is 7 per cent of GDP. Much of this is down to poor planning, poor management supervision, poor IT skills and low morale.

I have to hold my hands up here and say that my time management skills aren't the best. If I tell you otherwise I know the people who work for me will just fall about laughing. I'll admit that I'm not the best when it comes to time-keeping. Let's just say I'm working on it.

However, I still *try* to manage my time. I have an overall strategy, which is set out as follows:

First, I set a goal or a target – *eg* buy new property

Second, I work out how I am going to reach that target – *eg* write a business plan, use a team of investors to buy a property at auction

Third, I rent out the property at a monthly profit of X.

Not only do I have detailed business plans which outline each project, I plan each year and then I plan each month, each week and each day.

I keep a diary to help organise myself and I have a list of tasks for each day. and work through them. This helps keep me on track.

For me, one of the keys to time management is to try and not be fire fighting all the time. Fire fighting means dealing with things that demand your immediate attention, and in these, mini-crises come out of the blue and stop you doing other things such as planning ahead.

I want to be able to see what is coming up ahead, and I want my staff to know what is coming up ahead. That way we all know what we are doing, and when we are doing it for.

Marketing and Advertising

You could have the best in your business, but if nobody know about you, how are you going to get new business?

In a sense, even this book is part of my overall strategy to get better known. In an ideal world, the phone rings and all the business comes to you rather than you having to chase after it. This is what advertising and marketing does for you.

The cliché is always that word of mouth is the best form of advertising, which I agree with. But I also think you have to put in the leg-work to get to that stage. When I am looking for properties, that might mean printing flyers and getting them out under people's noses.

Anything that gets the word out there is the key. Nowadays everybody is using social media to the same ends – Twitter, Facebook, You Tube – or using search engine optimisation (SEO) to get your website higher than your competitors'. The process is very much the same, letting people know that you are open for business.

Ultimately you are aiming to create brand awareness, so that not only do people think of you when searching for that certain thing, they think of you first.

As part of my team I have freelance designers for print and for the web. There are lots of people out there who specialise in these kinds of business if you aren't the most technology-savvy person.

The marketing mix

The **marketing mix** is an idea among many marketing professionals that the best way to promote a product is to make people aware of it through various means. Gone are the days when we all read one evening newspaper or watched one TV channel.

There are so many ways in which we can advertise nowadays. The internet has changed the way in which we do so much of our buying. Our High Streets are changing to reflect this.

So whatever the business, you need to have a good think about your target market.

- Who are they?
- How old are they?
- What do they read?
- How many hours a day do they spend on the internet?
- Do you need to do some market research to get to know your target market better?

Once you have defined your target market, it is time to get your marketing mix together to cover all elements of reaching it.

Let us say you have a product that appeals to young and old. Young people are more likely to use the internet, so let's get that website of yours high on the Google rankings by employing some search engine optimisation. By also adding some internet advertising on Facebook and Gumtree we create a flow of queries which will feed back to that website.

On the other hand, older groups might be targeted through more traditional means, such as advertising in the local newspaper and a local radio station. You might also know of an event that is happening in your local area which you could sponsor – perhaps at a school, which reaches both age ranges?

LISTEN TO CRITICISM

Always keep an open mind and remain humble: don't be too proud to accept criticism. Critics point to our weaknesses. Obviously too much criticism can be destructive, and if you have a strong critic in your organisation, then be careful. But a certain degree of criticism is healthy, and is to be preferred over creating a culture of 'yes men' or people who just tell you what they think you want to hear.

Listen to everyone
Again, always try and find the time for people. I have had so many nuggets of information from the most unlikely of sources. Never turn your nose up at people. I have had old friends and tenants approach me in the street to tell me of a friend's property that I might be interested in – the sort of information I otherwise have to pay for.

Always be grateful and reward people who help you. This is the best way to ensure they will be prepared to help you again, and they will spread the word, too.

I'll come back to you
Those around me will be very familiar with this phrase I use as from time to time if I am presented with a proposition or query. Rather than provide an immediate response, I sometimes like to take time to digest the information so that I in turn can provide a suitable, solid response.

Always be yourself and follow your passion
This sounds obvious, but business takes us to unexpected places and sometimes puts us in contact with people with different backgrounds. I have felt intimidated in the past by some people, conscious of my accent and background. But as I have got older I have more faith in who I am and what I am about. I urge you to be the same, have faith in yourself and others will have faith in you.

Going into business can take us on quite a journey. We have to overcome our backgrounds and our weaknesses to push ourselves on to these new pastures. The good news is, you are not alone. There are lots of people who have gone before us, and there are lots of incredible stories out there that serve to inspire us to reach greater heights.

FINDING INSPIRATION

I have been thinking about writing this book for a while. I wanted to explain to people what I do, how I do it and most importantly *how you can do it too*. I feel it is time for me to give something back, and this book is part of that.

But I didn't think it was enough to just to say: 'OK, do abc and then xyz and Bob's your uncle!' The truth is I have had to push myself mentally by self-educating and have had to rewire much of the thinking that held me back in the past.

So as well as telling you some of the nitty gritty stuff, the nuts and bolts of making money from property investments, I want this section to be about something much more fundamental. Finding the strength inside yourself or **making it happen.**

MY INSPIRATION

Inspiration is a funny thing, and searching for it can take us on quite a journey. I can certainly say that my background and my parents were an inspiration to me. Watching them struggle and strive to get on definitely encouraged me to do the same. Even though I have now reached a position where I could take things more easy, I don't.

I could have stuck with building; plenty of builders have made a decent living. I could have stuck with running the building contractors; it was stressful, but it was a living. It is hard to explain what makes one person push on further and someone else stick with their lot. But most of getting ahead is quite simple: it just comes down to things like dreaming big, overcoming fear, believing in yourself and going for it.

That makes it sound easy, and I know it isn't. As I have just said, I have had to retrain my own thoughts to become much more of a 'go-getter'. I now know that the biggest things in our way are usually our own heads. But that's enough about me. It's time for *you* to take a look in the mirror.

WHAT IS YOUR INSPIRATION?

The first thing I want you to do is think hard about what *your* inspiration is.

Your inspiration might be very different from mine. Maybe you are working hard for someone else and feel as if they are profiting more from your work than you are. Or maybe you are working and you feel invisible – you are just a cog in a machine, nobody would notice if you left, nobody will notice if you stay. Or perhaps you have children and can see that there is no pot of gold for them (or you) at the end of the rainbow!

I'm talking about pensions, of course. The days of a guaranteed decent pension are long gone, and we have to think about making our own plans for retirement these days.

It is also quite possible in these times that you are facing redundancy. We are living in an uncertain age, when there is a great deal of change in the air. How we deal with change is what can lead us to success or failure.

Negative forces such as these are natural and normal. The important thing is to harness these feelings or changes as a springboard for action in a positive direction.

Don't let negative feelings take a hold in your life, don't accept that we must trudge on regardless. This is the sort of thing that makes people ill. (Remember I told you about when my hair fell out; what more of a sign than that do you need that changes are needed!) I am sure we have all worked with disillusioned people who hate their work and hate the company. Deep down they probably hate themselves for not actually *doing something* more fulfilling with their lives.

Don't become one of the '*If only I had…*' brigade. Be the captain of your own ship and steer your life and that of your family in a new direction – a direction where you are the boss, and you call the shots. You don't need to become Richard Branson to achieve financial freedom – just a willingness to go for it!

So what *is* holding you back?

WHAT'S YOUR EXCUSE?

As human beings we should never stop learning, never think that we know it all. There is always something new to learn and there is always someone out there who will have done something bigger, better or more beautiful than us. All we can do is strive and try and make the most of our lot. And that is not the same thing as settling for our lot!

One of the most common reasons I hear people say they won't leave their job and try another way of making money is that they **can't afford** to. It doesn't matter if you don't have any money. I started with nothing and many other successful businessmen started without any backing. We are almost conditioned to think that we shouldn't try and make a success of our lives. Especially in Britain, and especially if you are female... or black... or young... or old!

But I know this isn't true. I have helped lots of people get on the property ladder and make themselves a good little business. All kinds of people, people with more academic qualifications than me, people older than me. This is one of the great bonuses of the property business: it is open to all.

When people say they can't afford to, apart from being an excuse, it is also being short-sighted. You may have to stretch yourself financially, but in the long run you will be creating money for your future. So is it actually true that you can't afford to? Isn't it more likely, as I've said before, that you can't afford *not* to.

I know you can create a better financial future. There are lots of books out there which promise to change your life. I don't want to make it sound like I have a magic wand. Only you can change your life. I can certainly show you the tools you need, but only you can pick them up and use them to create something.

In this book I hope I have given you as much encouragement as I can, and I can also tell you what encourages me.

I am the kind of person who believes that if there is a will, there is a way. I know lots of normal people with normal jobs and normal incomes who have transformed their financial prospects.

I have made some good money out of property, and although I wouldn't say it was easy, it is a sight easier than when I worked as a carpenter or on a building site.

Make a promise to yourself that you will ditch the excuses. You might not immediately be able to turn off that **inner critic,** but let's commit to making a change. Let's take a positive step forward.

UNDERSTANDING FEAR

What holds us back? In most people I know it has been those little voices in our heads that tell us we can't do things. You don't have to be certified insane to hear voices in your head – we all get them. But it isn't just that 'inner critic' voice we get that puts doubt in our mind; there is more.

We are conditioned not to **take risks**. Think back to when we were children, and natural risk takers. Our poor old parents, thinking we were going to do ourselves harm, warned us against danger at almost every turn. 'Watch where you are going'; 'Be careful what you say'; 'Think about what you are doing'.

Anyone who is a parent will know that these words are delivered with the best of intentions, but we do have an exaggerated fear of 'danger'. The Government does a similar thing, and we now live in what in the UK is called by some 'the Nanny state', as there always seems to be someone who thinks they know what is best for us. The health and safety brigade, the council, your teachers at school, your workmates.

The media are perhaps the biggest communicators of negativity. The news deals with the 'here and now' and will always tell us when 100 more jobs have gone. Negative news values explain why the press and broadcast media are always full of bad things.

All these daily messages, from all these sources, put ideas into our head about what is 'normal' and should or shouldn't be done.

Again, the important factor is how you deal with these doubts and fears. Of course we need a bit of doubt to make us aware of danger, but once we have assessed that danger, we need to remain on course and go for it.

Think of these things as hurdles to jump. The first time you jump a hurdle your trainer will set the bar low, then a little bit higher. I propose the same: start with a height you are comfortable with and we can press on from there.

Have the confidence to trust in your gut instinct: if you think there is a better future out there, then there *is*. Let's go and get it!

CARRYING ON THE SAME

Often the worst thing we can do is nothing. if your instincts/subconscious/ambitions are bugging you, telling you to move on to new horizons, then why ignore them?

More often than not it is what we DON'T do that we end up regretting, more than what we DO. To do something and fail won't eat away at you half as much as not trying in the first place.

FINDING PURPOSE

Why don't I take things more easy? The answer is simple. The property business is what I love to do. I love to make deals with people. I love to see things happen and change, like a derelict house transformed into a home for someone. I also like to see things happen for other people. I am not as selfish as some business people out there. I believe there is enough to go around and the whole community can benefit from individuals creating a stronger financial bedrock for themselves.

When you find your purpose, motivation comes naturally.

THINGS FALL INTO PLACE

There is another odd phenomenon I would like to try to explain. When you step out of your comfort zone and start a new venture, things happen. You meet new people, your hear new information, you gain a new confidence.

If you sit in one position and think 'That will never happen', you are right in the one sense. It will never happen if you stay in the same position. But if you strive and take a risk, somehow the missing links will fall into place.

Remember the expressions 'Fortune favours the brave' and 'Nothing ventured, nothing gained'. Both are clichés for good reason.

IGNORING DOUBT

Doubt is just another way of fear manifesting itself. There is a book called *Feel the Fear and Do It Anyway*, by Susan Jeffers. I've not even fully read it, but I love the title so much I just think of that and go for it!

It's like doing a parachute jump: everything in our minds and bodies is shouting NOT to do it. But if you can get past that, if you can push yourself into new territory then the world is the same but also slightly different, you have grown a little bit more.

I DON'T HAVE AN ALARM CLOCK!

The worst thing anyone could ever buy me would be an alarm clock. I don't need it. I am so excited to get up each morning and get out and find what the day brings. Some people think I am mad, but seriously, wouldn't you love to be the same? I believe you can. You just need to find a purpose to your life and the motivation to make it happen.

HOW CAN I IMPROVE MY MOTIVATION?

If motivation is a sticking point for you, let's go back to basics and ask ourselves a few simple questions.

- *What do I enjoy doing?*
- *If money wasn't an issue, what would I do with my time?*
- *What am I good at?*

Answer all these questions honestly. Don't just sit there nodding your head, get a pen out and make a list. Remember the bit where I said about working? Well, that includes working on yourself! There is always room to improve, whoever you are and whatever you have achieved so far in life.

For me, I enjoy doing business and know that I am good at it. I am not good at every aspect of it, I readily admit that, and nowadays I employ people to do things for me such as keep the office ticking over, or look after the books. I also employ lots of tradesmen to renovate and maintain my properties for me. I don't claim to be a superhero, and I'll say it again: you need good people around you.

One of the first things to do when improving your motivation is to set yourself a goal. Not just any goal, but a **SMART** goal....

SPECIFIC
Can your goal be broken into smaller goals?

MOTIVATIONAL
Is your goal emotionally charged? Do you have the energy to carry out your goal?

ACCOUNTABLE
Can your goal be measured? When will you know you have achieved it?

RESPONSIBLE
Are you keeping within your own ethics and boundaries?

TOUCHABLE
Will you be able to touch something tangible once you have achieved your goal?

PLANNING

All of the above is useless without a decent plan. My plans tend to be simple. I write lists, every day I write a list. A simple list of what I want to get done that day.

In my mind I will have a larger goal in mind: complete such-and-such a project. But that large goal needs to be broken down into the many small jobs that will help me get to where I want to go.

Let's look at the steps to owning a property...

Finance   (small steps – speak to banks)
Research   (small steps – check websites, speak to agents)
Make an offer   (check your finances, speak to your agents)

SET TARGETS

Not only do I write a plan for every day, I also write down what I want to achieve. This can be a smaller project, such as writing this book, or a set of targets for the year.

I think that once you have achieved a target, you recognise this and you should **reward yourself**. I usually treat myself to a new shirt or something like that. It is important to do this, as it keeps you feeling good (and looking good, hopefully), and reminds you why you are pushing yourself along this path.

MAKING A BUSINESS PLAN

An important part of the planning process is writing your business plan. If you want to borrow money from a bank to give you that capital for your property or any other business idea they won't take you seriously without one. It is a common currency in the business world, but not difficult to do well.

First, think like the bank: they will want to make sure it all adds up. But it isn't just the sums. Prove to them that you have also checked out the following…

Market Research
Is your idea sustainable? Have you checked the market to make sure?

Who is the competition?
Is the market already crowded or have you spotted a gap?

Who will do what in the business?
Are you intending to do all the work yourself? Can you afford to pay a team of people to help you?

Do the sums add up?

Are there running costs? For an office, for example:

- When and how much will people be paid?
- How do you expect to manage cash flow

DON'T TAKE NO FOR AN ANSWER

This is a bit of a cliché, but I stand by the power of persistence. There are millions of examples of success coming after lots of rejections or failures.

Richard Branson has had several failures in his time; on one occasion he needed his mum to bail him out and much later, he had to sell Virgin Records to fund his failing airline.

I have seen it happen so many times; people think something can't be done and walk away. Often it is just a matter of being creative, and what looks like a locked door simply needs an extra bit of thinking for it to be unlocked.

When people say that something 'can't be done', it is often an excuse for not wanting to do something because it is difficult. Another reason for not wanting to do something is often rooted in fear of failure or a fear of change.

We are coming back to motivation again here, and the reason you are here in the first place and reading this book is because you are hoping to make a change.

I am a big fan of Bev James, who has written a best-selling book called *Do It or Ditch It*. Her message is a simple one: change comes about through action, not words. Just buying this book isn't enough. You need to read it, learn from it, absorb the information – but most important, put it into practice.

THE SLIGHT EDGE

A great inspiration to me has been Jeff Olson's *The Slight Edge,* a book that is now also on CD. I listen to it in the car each day on my way to work. It gives me inspiration and motivation to push on. His philosophy is simple; the best ideas always are.

Simple disciplines, repeated over time, create success. Simple mistakes, repeated over time, create failure. That is the crux of *The Slight Edge* principle. The example he uses which illustrates his point perfectly is this: if you eat a burger and fries today, you won't become unhealthy. But if you eat a burger and fries *every* day, then you will.

The Slight Edge is about controlling small everyday routines that have a compound impact over time.

Olson also says 'what is easy to do is also easy not to do'. Watching TV in favour of reading a book is another habit he urges us to change. He suggests if you can read just 12 books a year, one a month, then you are actually gaining hundreds of years of knowledge.

In my life I try and use Olson's *Slight Edge* by thinking what small things I can do that will make a big difference over time. So I have started reading more, reading books that challenge me and push me to think about things differently. I mainly read business books and self-improvement books, but I also get a lot out of sport, which I shall talk more about later.

INVEST IN YOURSELF

The world of business never stands still; there are constant innovations, and market conditions change. We also change, and what was initially difficult for us becomes easier as we get more familiar with what we are doing.

Training courses not only teach us the skills we need to be able to compete, they act as a refresher, a chance to recharge our batteries, in the same kind of way that a holiday would. We can see how other people in the industry do things, what is currently 'best practice', and we can bring some of those tips into the way we do things.

I have also worked with business coaches who can help you focus on the issues inside yourself which might be holding you back.

LEARNING FROM OTHERS – SOME INSPIRATIONS

What do all these people have in common: Richard Branson, Steve Jobs, Bill Gates and Duncan Ballantyne? Business success, of course, but something else. They all either dropped out of education (Gates, Jobs) or left school with few qualifications (Ballantyne, Branson).

Steve Jobs

Steve Jobs is celebrated as the founder of an iconic brand, Apple. There are a couple of things I really admire about him. I love the simplicity of Apple products and their brand statement from a few years ago, 'Think Different'. But I also like it that Jobs made no secret of the fact that he relied on intuition in many of his business dealings.

Sometimes things just don't 'feel right', you can't put your finger on it. The figures might stack up, everything looks good on paper. For me, I have had occasions where it might just be a property that feels 'wrong'. I often think if it feels wrong to me, it will feel wrong to potential buyers or letters and will give it a wide berth – or at the very least get a second opinion.

Jobs, like Branson, was the king of reinvention. Never settling on one idea, he was always convinced there was more: more inventions, more ideas, more profit!

Another attribute he possessed was incredible focus. Once he settled upon a product he went through hell and high water to get it realised, often being ruthless in the process. I wouldn't suggest I am as ruthless as Jobs, but I have made some very tough decisions and often these turn to our favour. Fortune favours the brave, as they say.

Richard Branson

Richard Branson is an interesting guy. At first he seems quite posh and you might think a business career was an obvious choice for him, but in real life he has dyslexia and found school really hard going. He left at sixteen with few qualifications to his name, very much like myself.

Even though his early ventures were successful on a small scale, his first Virgin record shop ran into trouble and his mother had to re-mortgage the family home to bail him out. Not a great way to start your business career, but he did what any self-respecting budding entrepreneur would do. He tried again.

There is another story that Branson was forced to sell Virgin Records for £500 million to keep Virgin Airlines afloat. Apparently after the sale was completed he cried, as he was out of the music business which had made his fortune.

Although sad, I like this story as it demonstrates that sometimes we have to make really tough decisions in business. But life has a funny way of putting challenges in our way and making us fight for what we want, making us stronger in the process. Branson fought back and eventually got back into the music business with V2.

Branson cites the keys to the success of the Virgin brand as 'informality and information'. That, plus keeping the organisation bottom-heavy and not having a huge number of managers. The other key factor to learn from Branson is diversification – never leaving all your eggs in one basket and not getting too emotionally attached to any one business.

Muhammad Ali

When I was growing up in the Sixties and Seventies all the young black guys wanted to be Ali. And who wouldn't? He had so much grace, power and wit. Ali inspired me to get into boxing, which I did from 12 to 14 years old. It taught me a lot about life, much of which I still hold close today.

Discipline
I had to train hard to box; if you were weak you'd get knocked down easily. In business I work hard to keep ahead of the game.

Take a few knocks
You can't box and expect to come away unscathed. It is similar in business. If you are in business you are probably going to make mistakes and lose some money. The trick is to get up and get back at them before you get knocked down for good!

Control

Ali was a master of control in the ring. He could play the long game and let opponents tire themselves out as he famously did with Foreman in the Rumble in the Jungle in 1974. You also need to control your emotions. I noticed very quickly that the more you got mad, the more you got hit. And I didn't like getting hit!

Inspiration from sport

I have always enjoyed sport, and have learnd a lot from it. Of course, I know not everyone is interested in sport, so please bear with me if you are one of those people. Hopefully, you will still appreciate the reasoning behind this.

So what lessons for business can we learn from sport?

Believe in yourself, even if nobody else does

Ian Wright was a striker for Arsenal back in the 1980s, and he is still in the public eye as a TV presenter. I was always struck by his positive attitude, and he has never changed that. I know people who have played golf with him and they say he is always the same, always wanting to win.

At the start of his career no professional clubs were interested in signing him; undeterred, he carried on playing non-league and Sunday league football and was eventually spotted and signed by Crystal Palace before moving to the big time at Arsenal.

Seize the opportunity when it comes

Opportunities don't sit and wait until you are ready to do something. There is that 'window of opportunity', and you have to go for it while you can. Using football again, look at the great opportunistic goal scorers – Gary Lineker, Michael Owen, Alan Shearer, Jimmy Greaves before them.

The one thing they all had in common was the ability to be clinical. So many footballers think they have scored before they have, and send their shots wide of the mark. A true goal scorer is strong

– not always of massive stature – determined and ready to take his opportunities when they arise.

Find the system that works for you

There are lots of great football managers out there, but the ones that interest me are the guys who really get the best out of footballers who may have fallen out of favour at other clubs. He has spotted something in the player that others have overlooked. Martin O'Neill is well known for doing this, but perhaps the best current example is Harry Redknapp.

Use the talent that is around you

Football is all about transfers and moving players around to create the perfect team, but sometimes you see a manager give an opportunity to a young player, often because he has no other choice because the rest of his players are injured. But that player comes on and makes such an impact that he breaks their way into the team. Wayne Rooney did this at Everton when he was just 16 years old.

Thank the team

This is a classic of sports people, and although it is a cliché, even great individuals need their team around them to help them achieve their best. Tennis is one of the ultimate solo sports, but Andy Murray struggled to find his best form without a coach. Now he has Ivan Lendl on board, many believe he will now start to fulfil his promise.

Be thankful for the luck

Much of life is a down to luck. They say you create you own luck. I don't really believe in fate or destiny, but I stay thankful for the luck and hope that it never runs out. Lots of footballers when asked about the winning goal will just say that they were in the right place at the right time.

Final word on inspirations

There are lots of people who are less well known who can offer us important business lessons.

Jeff Olson's *The Slight Edge*, mentioned earlier, reminds us that it is small behaviour patterns repeated consistently over time that can mark us apart from our competitors. Back to his enthusiasm for reading, he suggests we should read just 10 pages of a good book a day. It isn't the 10 pages that makes the difference, it is the 12 books a year that they add up to. Twelve books can really change our perception and our knowledge and give us that *slight edge* we are looking for.

Bev James's *Do it or Ditch it*, does as it says on the tin. This book reminds us that it is **action** that makes the difference to our lives.

Napolean Hill's *Think and Grow Rich* is a classic of self-help motivational business books. First published in 1937, it has sold a staggering 70 million copies, making it one of the best-read books of all time with its '13 rules for success'.

Final Word

The gist of all of these books is about getting into the mental attributes of successful people. Bristol might not be the centre of the universe, but there are lots of people in this city who have done very well for themselves – and I feel there is room for more. You don't have to be wealthy or well educated to be successful. You just need to believe you can achieve. Dare to dream a better life is possible – and remember, actions always speak louder than words.

Thanks for reading.

In order to succeed, your desire for success should be greater than your fear of failure
Bill Cosby

Genius is 1 per cent inspiration, 99 per cent perspiration
Thomas Edison

JARGON BUSTER

Property, like most trades and professions, tends to have its own language. Here is an explanation of some of the terms used in this book.

Auction
A purchase from an auction house rather than on the open market.

Below market value
Buying a house below the 'market rate'. Houses are often sold BMV with the aim of getting a quick sale.

Bridging loan
Interim finance for the purchase of a property until more permanent finance is obtained, usually by the sale of an existing property.

Buy-to-let
A mortgage aimed at people buying a second property specifically with the intention of letting it out to tenants.

Cash-back mortgage
When the borrower receives a lump sum from the lender on completion of the house sale.

Chain
The sale of one property often relies on the sale of another, so when one link breaks, the whole chain goes.

Equity
The difference between the mortgage value and the market value.

Effectively your mortgage is a loan, and when you have paid it off completely you own the house entirely.

Flexible mortgage
A flexible mortgage allows you to pay different amounts, such as repaying early, without being penalised.

Flipping
Flipping is the process of buying and selling a property quickly for a profit. This usually involves some cosmetic improvements to the property to help it sell quickly

Guarantor
This is someone – often a parent or grandparent – who effectively guarantees to pay the mortgage to prevent someone defaulting on a loan.

HMO
Houses of multiple occupancy – very often properties divided into flats.

Interest-only mortgage
A mortgage where only the interest is being paid to the lender and the full cost of the property loan remains.

Inventory
When letting a property to tenants, a list is made of all its contents. In a furnished property this will be everything from the settee to cutlery. When a property is vacated, the inventory should be checked before the tenant's deposit is returned.

Joint tenants
When two or more people appear on the tenancy agreement of a property: traditionally married couples and partners, these are now increasingly groups of friends.

Joint venture
A group of people such as investors or a family pooling their
resources together to buy a property.

Lease option
A contract between property owner and investor/tenant giving the
tenant an option to buy the property from the owner in a number of
years' time.

Mortgage term
The period of time over which a mortgage is repaid, traditionally 25
years but nowadays often 30 years.

Negative equity
When the mortgage is higher than the market value of the house.

Open market
Applies to houses for sale by estate agents, now invariably advertised
on the internet as well as locally.

Open market value
The price a buyer and seller agree a property is worth. When the
market was very strong, it was not unusual to see a house sell for
more than its open market value.

Private sale
An agreement between seller and buyer, normally with no Estate Agent.

References
Letters or emails for character and/or credit referencing from a
tenant's previous landlord or employer.

Repossession
When the occupier of a property is evicted by the mortgage lender

because they have defaulted on repayments.

Second steppers
Second investment properties for people who typically have another property in which they currently live.

Self-certification mortgage
Often taken by self-employed people who cannot guarantee their income in the way a traditionally employed person can. It usually has a higher interest rate.

Shared ownership
When there are joint owners of a property, often the occupier and a housing association.

Solicitor
Legal professional who acts as a go-between between buyer and seller.

Stamp Duty
A government tax applied to all house sales, in which the percentage rate varies depending upon the value of the property.
Current rates are as follows:
0 per cent on properties below £125,000
1 per cent over £125,000 to £250,000
3 per cent over £250,000 to £500,000
4 per cent over £500,000

Tenancy agreement
The legal document which acts as a contract of agreement between a landlord and tenant.

Tracker-rate mortgage
A mortgage which follows the Bank of England base rate.

Under offer
The period of time when a buyer and seller have agreed a sale in principle but are waiting for contracts to be exchanged to make it legally binding.

Valuation
The open market value of a property as estimated by an estate agent, and agreed by the seller.

Yield
Percentage profit (gross) made by the landlord from the difference between the mortgage cost and the rental income. For instance, mortgage £500 per month, rental income £750 per month gives a profit of £250 (a 33 per cent yield). A good yield for the property after everything has been paid is normally 8% upwards.

FURTHER RESEARCH

You can never know everything, so always be on the search for fresh information and viewpoints. Books can go into greater depth on a subject, while TV is great for showing us visual ideas. You also need to keep in touch with what is going on, so newspapers and magazines can alert you to new trends.

TV PROGRAMMES

Property programmes are a good place to do some armchair research and learn from other people's mistakes. They are particularly good at the 'makeover' element of property, less good at the business elements. Given the nature of these programmes you can see a lot of nightmare scenarios, learn from them but don't assume that property developing is as bad as they make it look! Programmes include:

- *Homes under the Hammer,* BBC One
- *60 Minute Makeover,* with Julia Kendell, ITV
- *Location, Location, Location,* with Kirstie Allsopp and Phil Spencer, Channel 4
- Phil Spencer: Secret Agent, More 4 and other digital channels

BUSINESS INSPIRATION BOOKS

Robert Kiyosaki, *Cash Flow Quadrant: Rich Dad's Guide to Financial Freedom* (Plata Publishing, 2011)
Napolean Hill, *Think and Grow Rich* (Capstone, 2009)
Jeff Olson, *The Slight Edge* (Momentum Media, 2005)
Jinny Ditzler, *Your Best Year Yet* (Harper Element, 2006)
Susan Jeffers, *Feel The Fear and Do It Anyway* (Vermilion, 2007)
Stephen Covey, *The Seven Habits of Highly Effective People* (Simon and Schuster, 2004)

NEWSPAPERS

All the quality newspapers and middle-market tabloids have property sections which can give up-to-date tips and advice on national trends and the financial elements of property buying. Mortgage comparison tables in newspapers can be worth looking at.

There are also magazines which specialise in aspects of property such as buy-to-let, buying abroad or even advice on which mortgage to get.

Locally there is usually a wealth of information built around the advertising of properties for sale through local estate agents. In Bristol the Evening Post's homes advertising is run in conjunction with www.FindaProperty.com, while an effective rival publication is Bristol Property Live (www.Bristolpropertylive.co.uk)

WEBSITES:

The following websites are great for researching properties in your local area:

* www.rightmove.co.uk
* www.zoopla.co.uk
* www.primelocation.co.uk

APPS:

An increasing number of free apps are being released to make house hunting easier, and many For Sale signs now carry a QR code which you can zap with your mobile and immediately see all the details of the property. The Find a Property app seems to do the job well.

LANDLORD INFORMATION:

If you are becoming a landlord for the first time there are some official bodies that provide information and advice.

* NLA national landlords association: www.landlords.org.uk
* Residential Landlords Association: www.rla.org.uk
* A good source of information for landlords and tenants alike is the housing charity Shelter: www.shelter.org.uk

CONTACT ME

If you have been inspired by anything in this book and would like to get in touch for more advice, or if you have a potential business idea then I'd love to hear from you.

Email:
dbproperties@aol.com

Website:
www.delbrown.co.uk